PIANO • GUITAR • FOUR-PART VOCAL

A ☆ M ☆ E ☆ R ☆ I ☆ C

⊘ GOSPEL TOP FORTY ⊘

Southern Gospel's Best

Contents

A *J. Aaron Brown & Associates* Publication
in association with

HAL•LEONARD®
CORPORATION

7777 W. BLUEMOUND RD. P.O. BOX 13819 MILWAUKEE, WI 53213

Antioch Church House Choir

By DARRELL HOLT

Please let me sing in the choir, in the choir,_ Please let me sing in the choir; One old

man can't be all that bad;_ Won't you please let me sing in the choir!_
1. I guess you'd
2. One cloud-y

say he's a fix-ture, 'round_ town they all_ knew his name,_ And ev -'ry-time the church-
Sun-day_ morn-ing, I re-mem-ber it was rain-ing some,_ The church-bells rang, and ev-

_ bells _ rang _ Un-cle Jes-se, he up and came;_ He al-ways_
'ry-bod-y came, ex-cept_ Jes-se, he did-n't come; And ev-'ry-bod-y

sat_ in the ver-y same pew — hum-ming in a voice loud and rough, When it
start-ed get-ting wor-ried,_ but they fig-ured they'd_ start an-y how; —

2nd time to CODA ✛

Canaanland Is Just In Sight

By JEFF GIBSON

1. Mos-es led God's chil-dren, for-ty years he led them through the
2. 'Tho we walk thru val-leys, 'tho we climb high moun-tains, we must

cold and through the night. ____ 'Tho they said, "Let's turn back," Mos-es said, "Keep go-ing,
not give up the fight. ____ We must be like Mos-es, we must keep on go-ing,

Ca-naan-land is just in sight." ____ There will be no sor-row there in that to-mor-row,
Ca-naan-land is just in sight. ____

CHORUS

we will be there by and by. ____ Milk and hon-ey flow-ing,

there is where I'm go-ing, Ca-naan-land is just in sight. ____

Bring Me Out Of The Desert

By LOIS TATUM

Call Me Gone

By KENNY HINSON

RECITATION

You know, I've been called an awful lot of things in my lifetime, and "smart" wasn't often one of them. But I was smart enough one day to call Jesus Christ the Lord of my life, and I called it quits to a whole lot of sinning. And it's because of that commitment that some folks think it's funny and laugh and call me foolish.

But let them go ahead and laugh, 'cause you see, that doesn't really bother me at all. Because even a fool can see by the shape she's in that this old world's about to fall. But as long as I let Jesus call the shots, I've got nothing at all to fear. And when that roll is called up yonder, don't call me, 'cause I'm not gonna be here!

The City Comin' Down

Author and Composer
LAVANUL SHERRILL

1. Well,___ man has made___ a lot of things,_____ – – They
2. Well,___ get your things___ to - geth - er,___ And walk out___
3. Well, there's New York Cit - y, Chi - ca - go,___ At - lan - ta and

look so fine,___ – – They're build-ing so___ high up in the sky___ they will
through the land,___ You're gon - na go___ on the rock - y moun - tain,___ gon - na
Bal - ti - more,___ – There's___ Den - ver and___ Tal - la - has - see,___ you can

al - most___ baf - fle your mind;___ But ___ the time's gon-na turn, and they're all gon-na burn,___ and
cross on the des - sert sand;___ Well,___ Lot went___ down to ___ Sod - dom,___ but
name them___ by___ the score;___ I don't___ have a___ big in - vest - ment,___ no

no - where___ will be found,___ I'm gon - na be up in that
not old___ A - bra - ham,___ He was ___ look - in' for that cit - y___ that
man - sion___ way up town,___ But I've___ got one in that

CHORUS

John saw＿comin' down.＿ I'm not look-in' for a cit-y that's a-go-in' up,＿ but the

one that's com-in' down,＿ I'm not put-tin' my trust in the one that will crum-ble and

fall down to the ground;＿ But I'm head-in' for the one that the Lord has made＿and is

built e-ter-nal-ly sound,＿ I'm not look-in' for a cit-y go-

-in' up,＿ but the one that's com-in' down.＿

A Different Way

By JEFF GIBSON

1. Now, the wise men went a seek-ing for the Sav-ior had been born
2. From, a babe born in the man-ger to the Man of Gal-i-lee

- And they knew that old king Her-od was out to take a-way our Lord;
He healed the sick and saved the sin-ners,_____ and set the cap-tive free;

When they found the ba-by Je-sus, knelt be-side Him in the hay,
So, no mat-ter where you're head-ed, come to Je-sus to-day

Then they left .... a dif-f'rent way.
And you'll leave .... a dif-f'rent way.

Excuses

By HAROLD S. LEAKE

RECITATION

1. In the summer it's too hot
   And in the winter it's too cold;
   In the springtime when the weather's just right,
   You find someplace else to go;
   Well, it's up to the mountains or down to the beach
   Or to visit some old friend,
   Or just to stay home and kinda relax
   And hope some of the kinfolks will start dropping in.

2. Well, the church benches are too hard,
   And the choir sings 'way too loud;
   Boy, you know how nervous you get
   When you're sitting in a great big crowd!
   The doctor told you now, you'd better watch those crowds,
   They'll set you back!
   But you go to that old ball game
   Because you say it helps you to relax.

3. Well, a headache Sunday morning,
   And a backache Sunday night,
   But by worktime Monday morning
   You're feeling quite all right!
   Why, one of the children has a cold—
   Pneumonia, do you suppose?
   Why, the whole family had to stay home
   Just to blow that poor kid's nose!

   (Sing chorus)

4. Well, the preacher, he's too young
   Or maybe he's too old,
   The sermons, they're not hard enough
   Or maybe they're too bold;
   His voice is much too quiet-like;
   Sometimes he gets too loud;
   He needs to have more dignity,
   Or else he's way to proud.

5. Well, the sermons, they're too long,
   Or maybe they're too short;
   He ought to preach the Word with dignity
   Instead of stomp and snort;
   Why, the preacher we've got
   Must be the world's most stuck-up man!
   Why, one of the ladies told me the other day,
   "He didn't even shake my hand!"

   (Sing chorus)

Feels Alright

By RANDY BUXTON

God Bless The U.S.A.

Words and Music by
LEE GREENWOOD

MCA MUSIC PUBLISHING

God's Gonna Do The Same

By RONNY HINSON

He's Still Working On Me

By JOEL HEMPHILL

1. There real-ly ought to be a sign up-on my heart, "Don't judge him yet, there's an

un - fin-ished part." But I'll be per - fect just ac-cord-ing to His plan,

fash-ioned by the Mas-ter's lov-ing hand. He's still work-in' on me to

make me what I ought to be. It took Him just a week to make the moon and stars, the

I Bowed On My Knees And Cried Holy

Arrangement by
JIMMIE DAVIS

1. I dreamed of a cit - y called glo - ry so bright and so
2. I thought as I en - tered that cit - y my loved ones all knew me

fair, When I en - tered that gate I cried ho - ly; the
well, They showed me thru the streets of heav - en; such

an - gels all met me there; They car - ried me from
scenes too nu - m'rous to tell; I saw A - bra - ham,

man - sion to man - sion, and oh, what sights I saw! But I
I - saac, and Ja - cob, Mark, Luke, and Tim - o - thy, But I

I Know My God Can Do It

By JEFF GIBSON

1. Three He - brew boys were thrown in - to the fire,
2. They marched a - round the walls of Jer - i - cho,

Be - cause be - fore the king___ they would not bow;
They knew that they would fall,___ God told them so!

But they said, "Lis - ten, king, let it be known:
Just like He worked for them, He's work - ing now,

We serve a liv - ing God,___ we're not a - lone!"
My God will nev - er change,___ He has great pow'r!

I'm A Jesus Fan

By MIKE PAYNE

In My Robe Of White

By GENIECE SPENCER INGOLD

It Wasn't Rainin'
(When Noah Built The Ark)

By JOEL HEMPHILL

It's Out Of This World

By RONALD M. PAYNE

Jericho

Words and Music by ANN BALLARD
and BILL BOOHER

Jesus Is Your Ticket To Heaven

Words and Music by
ARCHIE JORDAN

1. You can buy a tick-et to Par - is, You can buy a tick-et to Rome; You can buy a tick-et to Swe-den, But you can't buy a tick-et to that heav-en-ly home. You see Je-

2. You can buy a tick-et for a boat, You can buy a tick-et for a plane; You can buy a tick-et for a sub-way, But you can't buy a tick-et for that heav-en-ly train. You see Je-

sus is your tick-et to heav - en, And Lord, it's gon-na be so nice!

John Saw

By SANDY KNIGHT

I Think I'll Read It Again

By SANDY KNIGHT

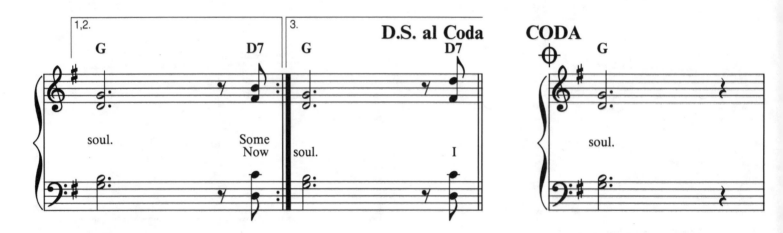

The King Of Who I Am

By TANYA GOODMAN
& MICHAEL SYKES

My days are filled with laugh-ter,____ my heart has known your

peace._____ I've tra-veled far,___ still there is far___ to go._____

_____ 'Cause in my heart there is a long-ing___ to look up-on Your

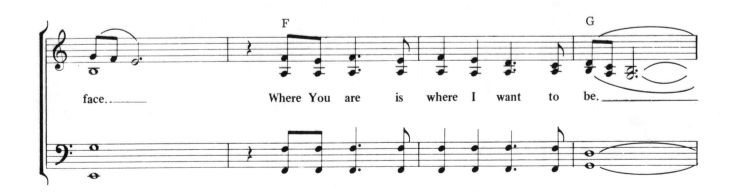

face._____ Where You are is where I want to be._____

2nd time Fine

Let Your Living Water Flow

By JOHN WATSON

CHORUS

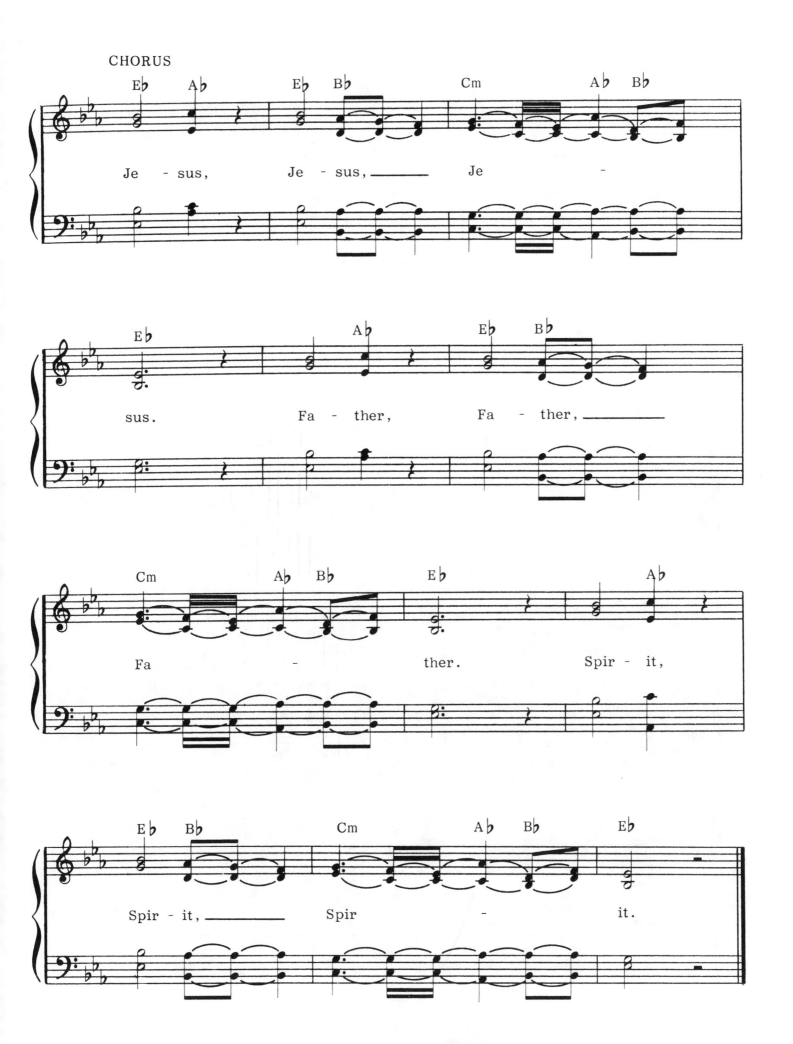

Man In The Middle

Words and Music by RON HELLARD,
BUCKY JONES and DAN WILSON

More Than Wonderful

By LANNY WOLFE

He pro-mised us___ that He would be a coun - sel - or a

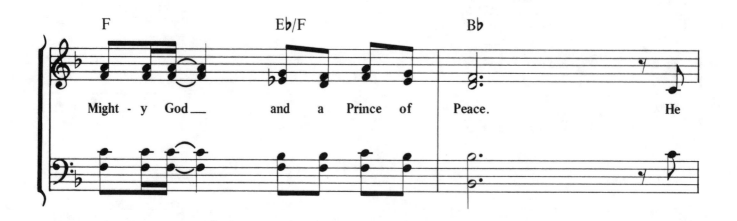

Might - y God___ and a Prince of Peace. He

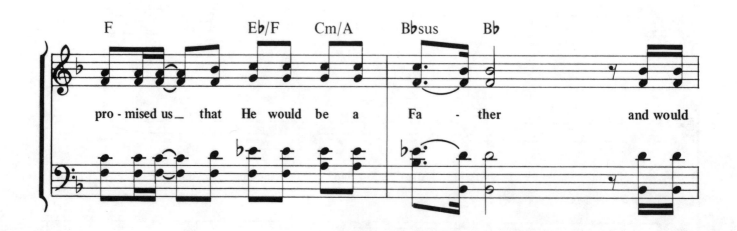

pro - mised us___ that He would be a Fa - ther and would

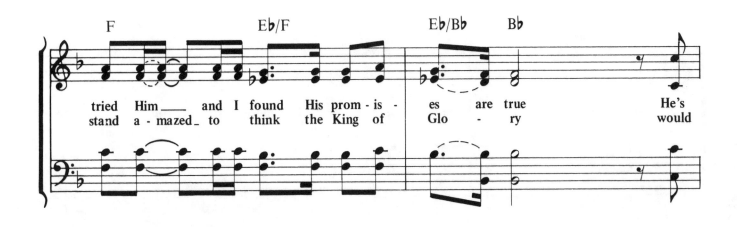

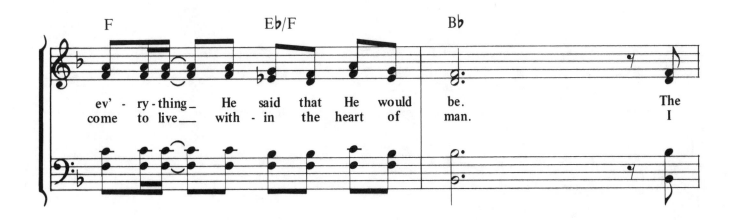

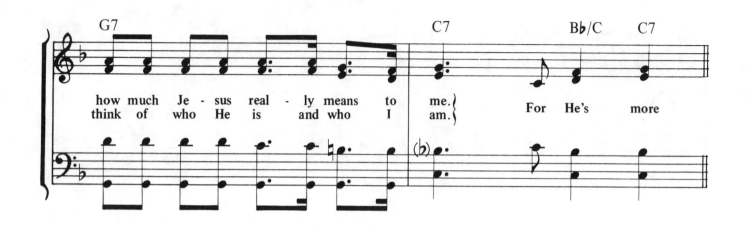

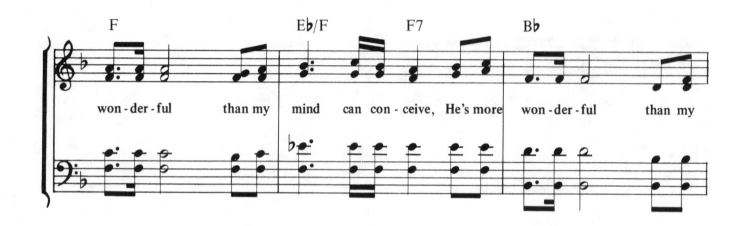

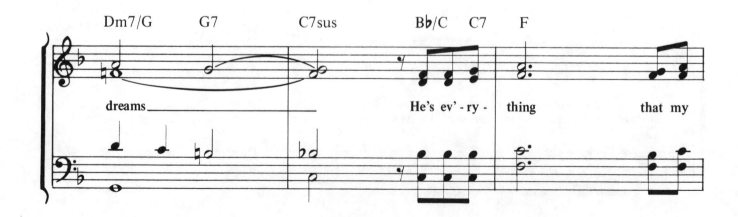

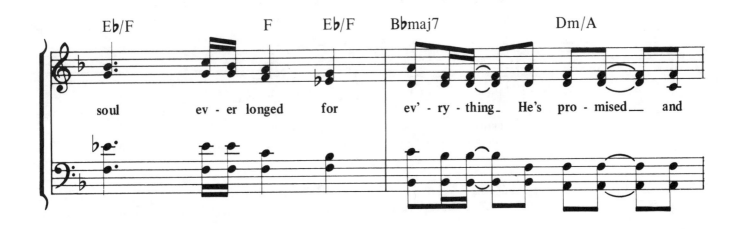

soul ev - er longed for ev'ry-thing He's pro - mised and

so much more. More than a - maz - ing more than mar - ve - lous more than mi -

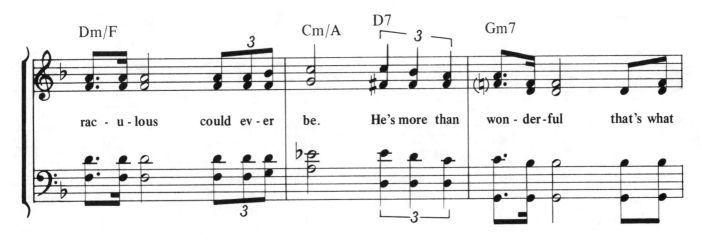

rac - u - lous could ev - er be. He's more than won - der - ful that's what

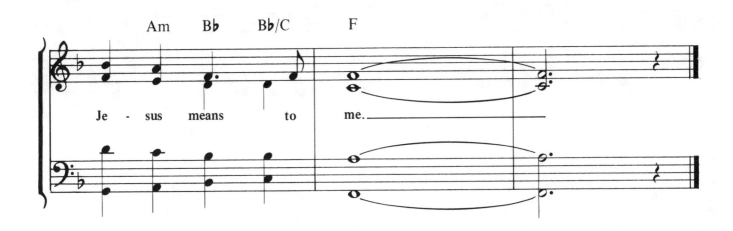

Je - sus means to me.

Moving Up To Gloryland

By LEE ROY ABERNATHY

CHORUS

won't e - ven be half way!
won't e - ven be   half   way!
and Hal - le - lu - jah Street.
and Hal - le - lu -   jah   Street.

Mov - ing,   moo - oo   oov - ing,
Oh, yes, I'm mov - ing, moving, mov - ing,   mov - ing,

mov - ing up to glo - ry - land,

Mov - ing,   moo - oo - oov - ing
Mov - ing, mov - ing, mov - ing,   mov - ing,

hold - ing to His nail-scarred hands;

Don't know when I'm leav - in', but I'm

read - y to go;   when I get to heav - en, I'll be   wel - come, I know,

Mov - ing,   Moo - oo - oov - ing,   mov - ing up to glo - ry - land.
Mov - ing, mov - ing, mov - ing,   mov - ing,

O For A Thousand Tongues

By DAVID BINION

An Old Convention Song

By TIM LOVELACE &
JERRY POWELL

1. We used to come from miles a-round, have dinner on the ground under-
2. Gos-pel songs to-day have a lot to say, they lift you

neath those old shade trees And sing the old songs in shaped notes, in
up when you're feel-ing down. Some have a coun-try fla-vor,

four part har-mo-ny; Like "He Set Me Free," and "He'll Pi-lot Me," and
some have a mod-ern sound. They all serve a need of plant-ing seeds, so I

"An-y-where Is Home." How long has it been since you heard an
know they can't go wrong But there's none so dear as when I hear an

Saints Will Rise

By CONRAD COOK

Somebody Touched Me

By SAVANA FOUST

65

Step Into The Water

By KIRK TALLEY

VERSES

1. It is time ___ we, the peo - ple, ___ stand up for what is right. It is time we squared our shoul - ders back, ___ raised ___ our swords to fight. ___ For the Bi - ble is our weap - on ___ and the Spir - it ___ is our shield, The ___ church needs more of its mem - bers to be work - ers in the field.

2. There is vic - t'ry for the Chris - tian ___ who walks the nar - row way, There has been a prize ap - point - ed for the soul ___ who does not stray. ___ Oh, I want to live for Je - sus, ___ be all ___ that I should be So that I can rest ___ with Him for - ev - er, live e - ter - nal - ly.

D.C.

Tarry Here

By JEFF MORAN

They're Holding Up The Ladder

By THE EASTER BROTHERS

1. As I climb this gos - pel lad - der al - ways heed - ing ev - 'ry sign,
2. There's a man - sion be - ing built for me some - where in glo - ry land,
3. -- Come on, you Chris - tian sol - diers, show the world your light can shine,
F7
Eb
Bb
-- I know my Sav - ior's with me, and He's teach - ing me to climb;
And this lad - der that I'm climb - ing is a part of the plan;
-- Get on this gos - pel lad - der and don't be a - fraid to climb;
Ev - 'ry day that I'm climb - ing there's a bat - tle for me,
I can hear the an - gels beck - on - ing, "Keep climb - ing, don't stop,
Can't you hear the an - gels cheer - ing soon the bat - tle will be o'er,
F7
Eb
Bb
Ev - 'ry step on this lad - der is an - oth - er vic - to - ry.
There's a crown of life a - wait - ing for you when you reach the top."
And we'll cel - e - brate the vic - t'ry when we reach that oth - er shore.

Two Winning Hands

By RONNY HINSON

CHORUS

Walk Right Out Of This Valley

By HAZEL TRUBEE

We Are Those Children

By JEFF GIBSON

1. They fled from E - gypt with old Pha - roah be - hind,
2. You may be walk - ing where it's dust - y and dry,

-- Hop - ing the prom - ised land soon they would find;
But soon we shall gath - er by the Riv - er of Life;

-- God's cho - sen peo - ple, they were will - ing to stand,
With saints of all a - ges we'll be sing - ing a - loud,

They would not give up till they reached that fair land.
We are those chil - dren God brought out.

CHORUS

We Shall Wear A Crown

Arranged by REX NELON

When He Was On The Cross

By RONNIE HINSON
& MIKE PAYNE

1. — I'm not on an e- go trip; I'm noth- ing on my own,
2. The look of love was on His face, — thorns were on His head,

Make mis- takes, I of- ten slip, just com- mon flesh and bones;
Blood was on His scar- let robe, — stained a crim- son red;

But I'll prove some- day just why I say I'm of a spe- cial kind,
— — Though His eyes were on the crowd, He looked a- head in time,

For when He was on the cross, I was on His mind.
And when He was on the cross, I was on His mind.

For He knew me, yet He loved me,

He whose glo - ry makes the heav - ens shine;

So un - wor - thy of such mer - cy,

Yet when He was on the cross, I was on His mind.

Who Put The Tears

By CAROL BASS

Thinkin' About Home

Words and Music by
TERRY TOLER